DISCOVER!

AMERICA'S AMAZING LANDMARKS

MARTIN LUTHER KING JR. NATIONAL MEMORIAL

By Marie Roesser

I0808709

Enslow PUBLISHING

Please visit our website, www.enslow.com. For a free color catalog of all our high-quality books, call toll free 1-800-398-2504 or fax 1-877-980-4454.

Library of Congress Cataloging-in-Publication Data
Names: Roesser, Marie, author.
Title: Martin Luther King Jr. National Memorial / Marie Roesser.
Description: New York : Enslow Publishing, [2026] | Series: America's amazing landmarks | Includes bibliographical references and index.
Identifiers: LCCN 2024054578 (print) | LCCN 2024054579 (ebook) | ISBN 9781978543959 (library binding) | ISBN 9781978543942 (paperback) | ISBN 9781978543966 (ebook)
Subjects: LCSH: King, Martin Luther, Jr., 1929-1968–Juvenile literature. | Martin Luther King, Jr., Memorial (Washington, D.C.)–Juvenile literature. | Washington (D.C.)–Buildings, structures, etc.–Juvenile literature.
Classification: LCC F203.4.M118 R64 2026 (print) | LCC F203.4.M118 (ebook) | DDC 917.53–dc23/eng/20250203
LC record available at https://lccn.loc.gov/2024054578
LC ebook record available at https://lccn.loc.gov/2024054579

Published in 2026 by
Enslow Publishing
2544 Clinton Street
Buffalo, NY 14224

Copyright © 2026 Enslow Publishing

Cover Designer: **Nicholas Switalski**
Interior Designer: Rachel Rising
Editor: Therese Shea

Photo credits: Cover, p. 1 ItzaVU/Shutterstock.com; Cover, p. 1, 5, 9, 11, 15, 21 Oleksandr Poliashenko/Shutterstock.com; pp. 1, 3-24 Jeffery Edwards/Shutterstock.com; p. 5 Peter Hermes Furian/Shutterstock.com; p. 5 Felix Mizioznikov/Shutterstock.com; p. 7 https://en.m.wikipedia.org/wiki/File:Martin_Luther_King_Jr_NYWTS.jpg; p. 8 https://commons.wikimedia.org/wiki/File:Martin_Luther_King,_Jr._National_Historic_Site_0034038-R1-E011.jpg; p. 9 https://en.m.wikipedia.org/wiki/File:March_on_washington_Aug_28_1963.jpg; p. 10 https://commons.wikimedia.org/wiki/File:IhaveadreamMarines.jpg; p. 11 https://en.m.wikipedia.org/wiki/File:Martin_Luther_King_-_March_on_Washington.jpg; p. 13 https://en.wikipedia.org/wiki/File:Lyndon_Johnson_signing_Civil_Rights_Act,_July_2,_1964.jpg; p. 15 Rey Rodriguez/Shutterstock.com; p. 17 Tada Images/Shutterstock.com; pp. 18, 21 kropic1/Shutterstock.com; p. 19 Dani Ber/Shutterstock.com.

All rights reserved. No part of this book may be reproduced in any form without permission in writing from the publisher, except by a reviewer.

Printed in the United States of America

Some of the images in this book illustrate individuals who are models. The depictions do not imply actual situations or events.

CPSIA compliance information: Batch #CSENS26: For further information contact Enslow Publishing, at 1-800-398-2504.

Find us on

CONTENTS

BOLDFACE WORDS APPEAR IN THE GLOSSARY.

IMPORTANT PERSON, IMPORTANT PLACE

A memorial is an object made to honor a person or event. The Martin Luther King Jr. National Memorial is in Washington, D.C. It honors Dr. Martin Luther King Jr. He was an important leader in the United States in the 1950s and 1960s.

THE MEMORIAL HONORS BOTH KING AND HIS WORK.

HIS LIFE AND WORK

Martin Luther King Jr. was born in Georgia in 1929. This was a time when many Black people faced **prejudice** in the United States. King became a Baptist **minister**. He taught that peaceful actions could change the world.

Martin Luther King Jr. in 1964

King and others worked for equal **civil rights** for Black Americans. For example, they wanted to end **segregation.** This was the practice of separating Black and white Americans in many areas of life, such as at school and on buses.

KING LED PEACEFUL PROTESTS, SUCH AS MARCHES.

King helped lead the March on Washington for Jobs and Freedom in August 1963. About 250,000 people marched for civil rights in Washington, D.C. King made a famous speech, called the "I Have a Dream" speech. King spoke of a future without **racism**.

KING'S POWERFUL WORDS THAT DAY ARE A PART OF HIS NATIONAL MEMORIAL.

In 1964, the Civil Rights Act passed. This law made some kinds of **discrimination** illegal. In 1965, the Voting Rights Act was passed. It protected, or guarded, Black Americans' right to vote. King was working for more changes when he was killed in 1968.

the signing of the Civil Rights Act

MAKING A MEMORIAL

In 1996, the U.S. government authorized, or approved, a memorial for Martin Luther King Jr. on the **National Mall**. More than 900 artists entered a contest for the memorial's design, or shape and look. A design was chosen in the year 2000.

THE MARTIN LUTHER KING JR. NATIONAL MEMORIAL WAS BUILT BETWEEN 2009 AND 2011.

PARTS OF THE MEMORIAL

Visitors enter the memorial through two towering stones. This is called "The Mountain of **Despair**." From there, visitors see another large stone ahead. It's called "The Stone of Hope." These names come from the "I Have a Dream" speech: "Out of the mountain of despair, a stone of hope."

The Mountain of Despair

On the other side of the Stone of Hope is a large **carving** of King. It's 30 feet (9.1 m) tall. A long wall around the memorial has 14 Martin Luther King Jr. quotations, or sayings. They're mostly about peace, equality, and love.

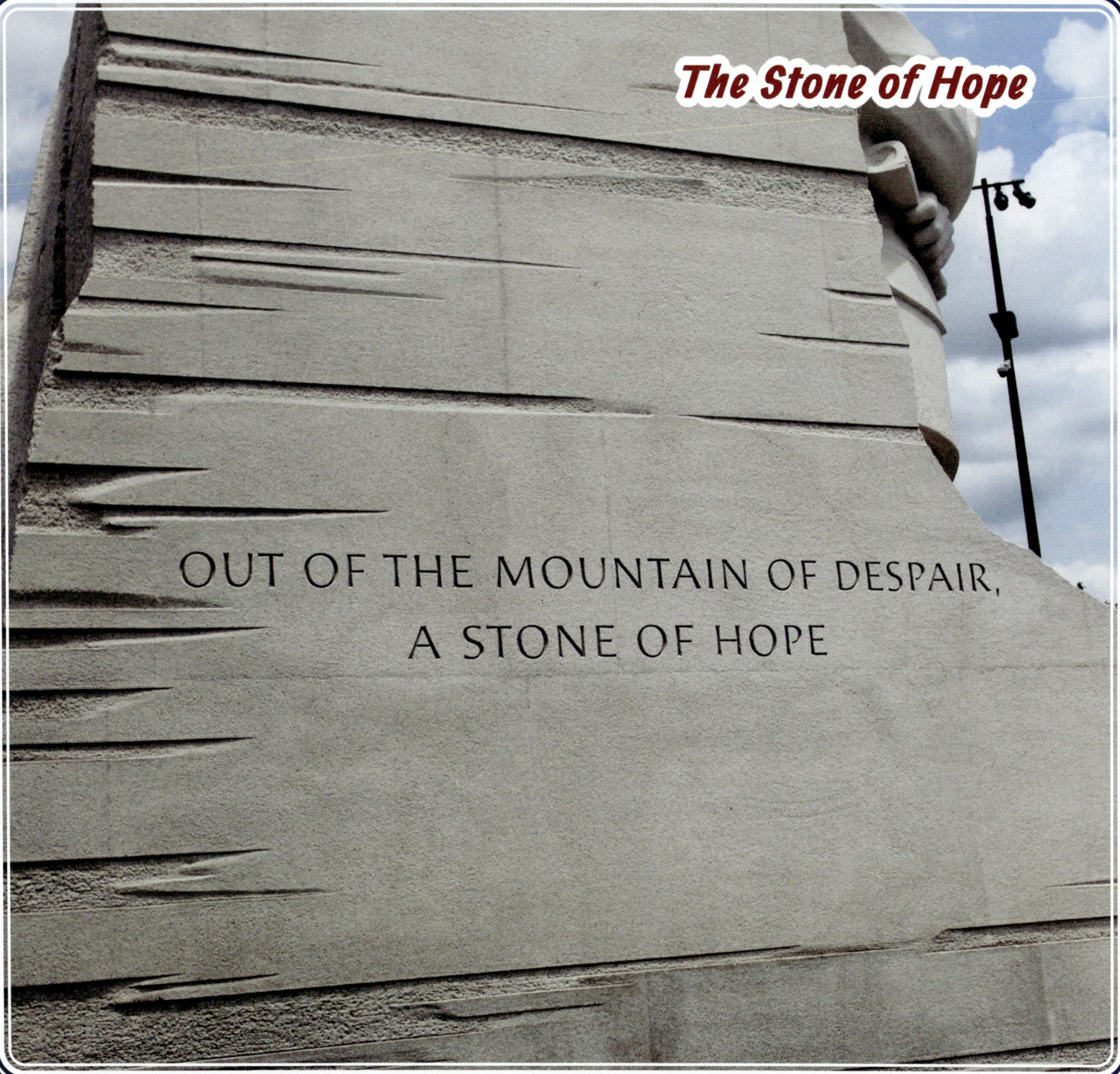
The Stone of Hope
OUT OF THE MOUNTAIN OF DESPAIR,
A STONE OF HOPE

VISIT THE MEMORIAL

Anyone can visit the Martin Luther King Jr. National Memorial. It's open 24 hours a day. It reminds us there is always hope for those in despair. It also reminds us one person can make a difference in the world, just as King did.

THE MARTIN LUTHER KING JR. NATIONAL MEMORIAL HELPS KEEP KING'S MEMORY AND MESSAGE ALIVE.

GLOSSARY

carving: Something cut into stone or another surface.

civil rights: The freedoms granted to us by law.

despair: The feeling of having no hope.

discrimination: Unfairly treating people unequally because of their race or beliefs.

minister: A person who leads a church service.

National Mall: A park with many monuments in Washington, D.C., the capital city of the United States.

prejudice: An unfair feeling of dislike for a person or group because of race or some other feature.

protest: An event at which a group objects to an idea, an act, or a way of doing something.

racism: The belief that people of different races have different qualities and abilities and that some are superior or inferior.

segregation: The forced separation of races or classes.

FOR MORE INFORMATION

Books

Rogers, Amy B. *Martin Luther King Jr.* New York, NY: Cavendish Square Publishing, 2022.

Santella, Andrew. *Martin Luther King Jr.: Civil Rights Leader.* Mankato, MN: The Child's World, 2022.

Websites

Martin Luther King Jr. Memorial
www.nps.gov/mlkm/index.htm
Read more about the memorial and the man it honors.

10 Facts About Martin Luther King
www.natgeokids.com/uk/discover/history/general-history/martin-luther-king-facts/
Find out more about King's life and work.

Publisher's note to educators and parents: Our editors have carefully reviewed these websites to ensure that they are suitable for students. Many websites change frequently, however, and we cannot guarantee that a site's future contents will continue to meet our high standards of quality and educational value. Be advised that students should be closely supervised whenever they access the internet.

INDEX